John F. Kennedy Library Foundation

JFK 100: Milestones & Mementos

Foreword by Caroline Kennedy

Text by Stacey Bredhoff
Curator, John F. Kennedy Presidential Library and Museum

JFK 100

The John F. Kennedy Presidential Library and Museum is one of fourteen Presidential Libraries
administered by the National Archives and Records Administration.

Book Design: Paul Montie
Editors: Mary C. Ryan, James Worsham, National Archives and Records Administration
Printed by Puritan Press, Hollis, NH

Cover photograph of John F. Kennedy ©Estate of Jacques Lowe

Foreword

On May 29, 2017 we celebrated what would have been my father's 100th birthday.

I have thought about him, and missed him, every day of my life. But growing up without him was made a little easier thanks to all the people who kept him in their hearts—who told me that he inspired them to work, and fight, and give back to this country that has given us all so much.

As my father becomes a part of history rather than living memory, the John F. Kennedy Presidential Library and Museum is committed to making his life and work accessible to future generations. The Library preserves mementos that help bring to life the family he grew up in and the family he made for us. It also preserves the documents and official records of his Presidency so that future scholars and interested citizens can research issues that still resonate in our public life—civil rights, nuclear disarmament, technology and innovation. In this Centennial exhibit, we chose one hundred artifacts—mostly from the Kennedy Library's collection—each of which helps tell his story.

My father's boyhood scrapbook shows a smart, yet mischievous student, struggling to get his academic bearings. The tattered flag of the PT 109 tells the story of a young Navy lieutenant who risked his life to save his crew. We can read the diary of a young congressman visiting a different part of the world to better understand America's role. We see the travel-worn suitcase of a presidential candidate, crisscrossing the country to listen and learn from the American people. A map made during the Cuban Missile Crisis reveals the high stakes as President Kennedy balanced resolve with statesmanship to avert a nuclear

catastrophe. His handwritten notes used for his televised address to the nation on civil rights show a president fighting for peace, justice, and a better world. And two small chestnuts—treasures from the White House lawn that my brother and I gave to our father—remind us of the humanity of our nation's leaders.

I remember hiding underneath his Oval Office desk and sitting on his lap on the Honey Fitz. He would point out the White Shark and the Purple Shark, who always followed the boat, although I could never quite see them. He said they especially liked to eat socks, and would have his friends throw their socks overboard—which I loved.

These are my family's stories. But every family has its own stories of that time. We hope that parents and grandparents will use this exhibit to recall their experiences—and share them with younger generations so they can better understand the experiences that informed my father's vision for our country, the values he championed, and the future he fought for.

President Kennedy inspired a generation that transformed America. They marched for justice. They served in the Peace Corps, in the inner cities, and in outer space. As my father said in his Inaugural Address, this work will not be finished in our lifetime. It is up to us to continue to pass on these chapters in our shared history—and the values that we cherish—to our children and grandchildren so that they may continue to seek a better world.

Caroline Kennedy
New York, 2017

JFK 100—Milestones & Mementos

One hundred years after his birth, John Fitzgerald Kennedy, 35th President of the United States, remains one of the most compelling figures of the 20th century. During the perilous days of the Cold War, and amid the rising dangers of the nuclear age, he delivered a message of hope to a nation that was hungry to hear it. He lifted the spirits of people around the globe with his courage and confidence. He gave strength to those suffering from oppression, hunger, and despair. He gave voice to the nation's noblest aspirations. And he galvanized a generation, as untold numbers of citizens answered the call to service that he issued with the words, "Ask not." Projecting a vision of a better world while affirming the country's founding principles of freedom and equality, he summoned the nation's citizenry to confront the great problems of the day.

President Kennedy's legacy speaks for itself. More than half a century after he established the Peace Corps, some 225,000 Americans have volunteered around the world—sharing, in the President's words, "the great common task of bringing to man that decent way of life which is the foundation of freedom and a condition of peace."[1] Eight years after JFK challenged the nation to land a man on the Moon within a decade—a seemingly impossible goal—two American astronauts left their footprints on the dusty lunar surface. JFK was the first U.S. President to define the issue of civil rights as a moral issue, marking a milestone in the modern civil rights movement. And in one of his most impassioned addresses, delivered in a city square of Berlin that now bears his name, he electrified the crowd of hundreds of thousands of Berliners, as he praised their courage and fortitude and championed the cause of democracy with words that endure today as a ringing defense of freedom: "Ich bin ein Berliner."[2] President Kennedy's speeches have entered the canon of American oratory; his grace and personal magnetism continue to captivate.

But a century after he was born, John F. Kennedy is known to many solely as a distant, historical figure. This book aims to make him known, less as an icon, and more as a man. One hundred items, drawn mostly from the collections of the John F. Kennedy Presidential Library and Museum in Boston, Massachusetts, are presented here, chronicling the life of the 35th President.

Although President Kennedy evolved into a polished, sophisticated, elegant, and eloquent statesman over the course of his life, these 100 items reveal some of the steps along the way. And while each of them tells its own story, they are also dots that connect to form a larger portrait of the man. The love of history and poetry and language that found full expression in a speech he gave as President dedicating the Robert Frost Library at Amherst College (see p. 88), is evident in his high school scrapbook in which the 17-year-old listed his favorite subjects, songs, and poems (see p. 15); the insights into international affairs articulated in a 1951 radio address that he gave as a young congressman returning from a seven-week tour of the Middle and Far East (see p. 30) reflect a world view that he would carry into the Oval Office a decade later;

and his first official act as President, signing an Executive Order increasing food allotments for the poor, was almost certainly informed by the hunger he witnessed first-hand and addressed in a speech during a Presidential campaign stop in the pivotal primary race in West Virginia (See pages 52-53).

There are several items in this book that speak to the majesty and dignity of the office of President that JFK so revered, but it is the everyday things that speak most poignantly of his humanity: the beat-up suitcase that he carried around the country throughout the 1960 Presidential campaign, the pencils from his desk and the pair of chestnuts that his young children found on the grounds of the White House.

These 100 items provide glimpses of the man, humanizing a monumental, yet elusive historical figure. One hundred years after his birth, they allow us to revisit his ideals and to deliver his timeless message of hope to a world that still yearns to hear it.

This book is based on a special exhibition that opened at the John F. Kennedy Presidential Library and Museum in Boston, Massachusetts, in May 2017 to mark the centenary of JFK's birth. The 100 items are numbered and presented, generally, in chronological order.

Boston Evening Globe

Evening Edition 1c
Closing Market Prices

VOL. XCI—NO. 149

BOSTON, TUESDAY EVENING, MAY 29, 1917—FOURTEEN PAGES

COPYRIGHT, 1917, BY THE GLOBE NEWSPAPER CO.

PRICE ONE CENT

EVENING EDITION—7:30 LATEST

BRITISH LOSE THREE SHIPS

Government After Draft Opponents

LONDON, May 29 — The British hospital ship Dover Castle has been torpedoed and sunk. It is announced officially.

The British armed merchant cruiser Hilarty also has been torpedoed and sunk, and a British destroyer has been sunk after a collision.

GERMANS ARE INDICTED

C. F. CHOATE JR ONE OF 16 DELEGATES

Chosen to Constitutional Convention

Arthur D. Hill of Boston Loses His Place on the Recount

COAL DEALERS PUT THE BLAME ON MINE MEN

Conference at the State House on Matter

Attorney General and the District Attorney Meet 19 Retailers

MACMILLAN SAFE IN GREENLAND

NEW YORK, May 29—Donald Macmillan, the explorer, and other members of the Crocker Land expedition, which went into the Arctic in 1913, are safe at Etah, on the northwest coast of Greenland, according to a cablegram received today by the American Museum of Natural History.

The cablegram announcing the whereabouts of the party, last heard from in July, 1916, was signed by Dr H. J. Hunt, surgeon of the expedition, who has reached the Faroe Islands, on his way to Denmark.

The message is as follows:

"Macmillan, Comer, Small and Hovey are at Etah. Steamer Denmark (the second relief ship sent after the Macmillan expedition) is at North Star Bay (150 miles from Etah). Ekblow, geologist, at Godhavn."

MESSAGE OF THE BOYS OF '61 TO THE BOYS OF '17

"We Carried the Flag Then; You Carry It Now"

"DO WHAT WE DID IN THE PAST"

Past Commander-in-Chief, G. A. R.

FRENCH VICTORY NEAR VERDUN

RED SOX PLAY DOUBLE-HEADER

Leonard Pitches Opener Against Senators

THE WEATHER

CLOUDY

Tuesday, May 29, 1917. News of the Day.

The United States is at war. Aging veterans who had fought in the Civil War call on a new generation of Americans to perform their duty to safeguard democracy: "We carried the flag then. You carry it now."[3] World War I, as the conflict came to be known, would claim the lives of millions of people around the world, including 116,000 serving in the U.S. military.[4]

Three years before American women would win the right to vote nationwide, the first woman elected to federal office, Jeanette Rankin of Montana, made the news from her seat in the U.S. House of Representatives, calling on women to support the national effort to conserve food. "Every Kitchen Must Be Mobilized," pronounced the headline inside the *Boston Globe*.[5]

An episode of mob violence targeting African American men, women, and children in East St. Louis, Illinois was reported in the *New York Times*.[6] Just over a month later, racial tensions again erupted into a major riot that lasted for days and drew national attention. The event was a precursor to similar explosions of racial violence in other American cities that set the stage for the modern civil rights movement.

Just six years after the U.S. Army had purchased its first airplane (built by the Wright Brothers), the War Department ran an ad to recruit student aviators.[7] The first successful non-stop transatlantic flight by the U.S. military was still two years away.[8]

And the Boston Red Sox, reigning world champions, were on their way to Washington, DC to play a double-header.[9] The team would lose the title in 1917, but win it back in 1918, after which fans would wait 86 long years to celebrate another Red Sox victory in the World Series.

While these topics filled the pages of newspapers on May 29, 1917, another event—whose impact on the 20th century would not be known for many years—took place at 3:00 p.m. in the second-floor bedroom of a family home on a tree-lined street in Brookline, Massachusetts: John Fitzgerald Kennedy was born.

Birthplace of John F. Kennedy, 83 Beals Street in Brookline, Massachusetts

John F. Kennedy Presidential Library and Museum

Courtesy *Boston Herald*

In 1914, newlyweds Rose and Joseph P. Kennedy settled into this seven-room home; they moved with their growing family to a larger house down the street in 1920.

1

Portrait from John F. Kennedy's first formal photo session, ca. November 1917

Photograph by Alfred Brown Studio,
Brookline, Massachusetts

John F. Kennedy Presidential Library and Museum

John –"Jack," as he was called by his family and close friends—was the second of nine children born into a close-knit, politically connected Irish Catholic family in Brookline. He had three brothers and five sisters, one of whom was born with an intellectual disability. Politics was in JFK's blood. Both of his grandfathers—sons of immigrants who came to the United States from Ireland to escape the potato famine in the 1840s—held elective office.

JFK's mother, Rose Fitzgerald Kennedy, was the daughter of John Francis "Honey Fitz" Fitzgerald, who served as a U.S. Representative and mayor of Boston. His father, Joseph P. Kennedy, an enormously successful businessman, would come to hold high government posts, including Ambassador to Great Britain. Both parents instilled in their children strong values of faith, family and public service, as well as a thirst for learning and a drive to succeed.

2

Health records of the Kennedy children, maintained by their mother

John F. Kennedy Presidential Library and Museum

The mother of nine, Rose Kennedy devised a card file system to track her children's health; she bought this cedar box in Brookline to house the records. On the card for Jack she listed whooping cough, measles, chickenpox, scarlet fever, mumps, German measles and bronchitis. On subsequent cards she chronicled an appendectomy, tonsillectomy, and the constant struggle to keep up his weight.

While Jack grew up with every material advantage, he suffered from a series of medical ailments that mystified his doctors and would continue to plague him as an adult. He learned to underplay the effects of his illnesses and, later, to hide the physical suffering he would endure throughout his lifetime.

"I purchased a card file from the stationers . . . and recorded all the important information about each of the children. It helped so much to be able to check back on the symptoms of illness, weight, diet and all the important information . . . I would recommend this idea to any mother."

–Rose Kennedy, mother of John F. Kennedy[10]

Kennedy children with their mother at Hyannis Port, ca. 1934-1935

John F. Kennedy Presidential Library and Museum

Left to right: Joe Jr., Jack, Rosemary, Kathleen, Eunice, Patricia, Bobby, Jean, Teddy, with Rose

3

"Plant a Tree," crayon drawing by John F. Kennedy, ca. 1929–1930

John F. Kennedy Presidential Library and Museum

JFK poses with three of his most mischievous high school friends, members of the secret "Muckers" club Jack organized while at Choate, ca. 1934

John F. Kennedy Presidential Library and Museum

Left to right: Ralph Horton, Lem Billings, Butch Schriber, and John F. Kennedy

While at Choate, the private boarding school in Connecticut he attended from 1931 to 1935, Jack distinguished himself with his keen intellect and winning personality, but his academic performance was uneven, as he applied himself only to the subjects he enjoyed. He was a disorganized student and a prankster, who was often in trouble with his teachers, parents, and school headmaster.

The headmaster's term for troublemakers was "muckers," which the group adopted and wore as a badge of honor. One of the Muckers' schemes, thwarted by the school headmaster before it could be executed, was a plan to move a pile of horse manure into the school gym; the idea nearly got the group expelled.[11]

4

Choate scrapbook, 1934—1935, selected pages

John F. Kennedy Presidential Library and Museum

Jack compiled this scrapbook while at Choate. There are several references to the Muckers, but in spite of his high-spirited antics, Jack's taste in poetry, as reflected on the page titled "My Favorites" (facing page) suggests a more sober-minded and fatalistic streak. He listed as his favorite poem "[I] Have a Rendezvous with Death," written by Alan Seeger, an American poet who volunteered in the French Foreign Legion and died in World War I at the age of 28. Published posthumously in 1917, the poem remained one of JFK's favorites throughout his life.

Selected pages from Jack's Choate scrapbook continue on the following 3 pages. Transcriptions and explanatory comments appear with each page.

"School begins—Oh God."

First Year

Study—Ancient History
Book—Botsfords [*George Willis Botsford and Lillie Shaw Botsford, authors of A Source-Book of Ancient History*]
Music—Love Locked out"
Sport—Football
Song—Love is the Sweetest Thing
Opera—Mikado
Actress—Ethel Merman, Claudette Colbert
Club—Mucks
Cozy Corner— "Sanctum"

Second Year—1933

Study—~~Physics~~ English
Song—Love Locked Out
Actress—Madge Evans
Pastime—Beefing
Club—East Cottage Club
Cozy Corner—Sanctum

Fourth Year—1935

Study—English History
Poem—Have a Rendezvous with death
[*"I Have a Rendezvous with Death,"
by Alan Seeger*]
Music—Melody of Broadway
Actor—Clark Gable
Society—Mucks
Actress—Claudette Colbert
Pastime—Beefing
Club— "Muckers"
Cozy Corner—West Wing 215
[*Choate dormitory*]

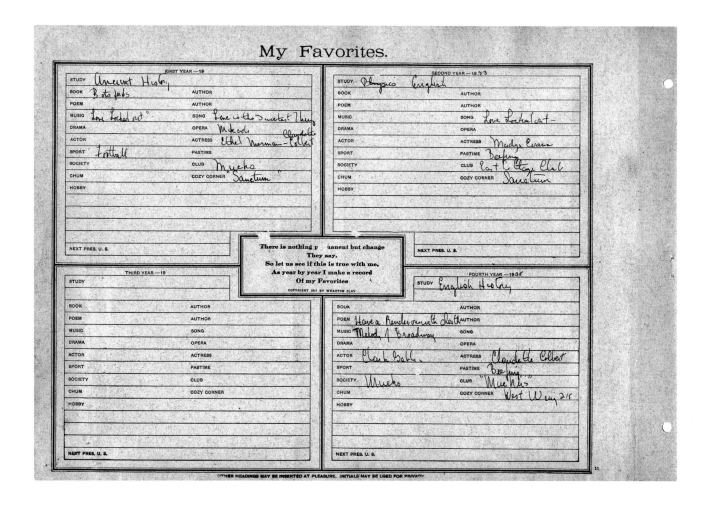

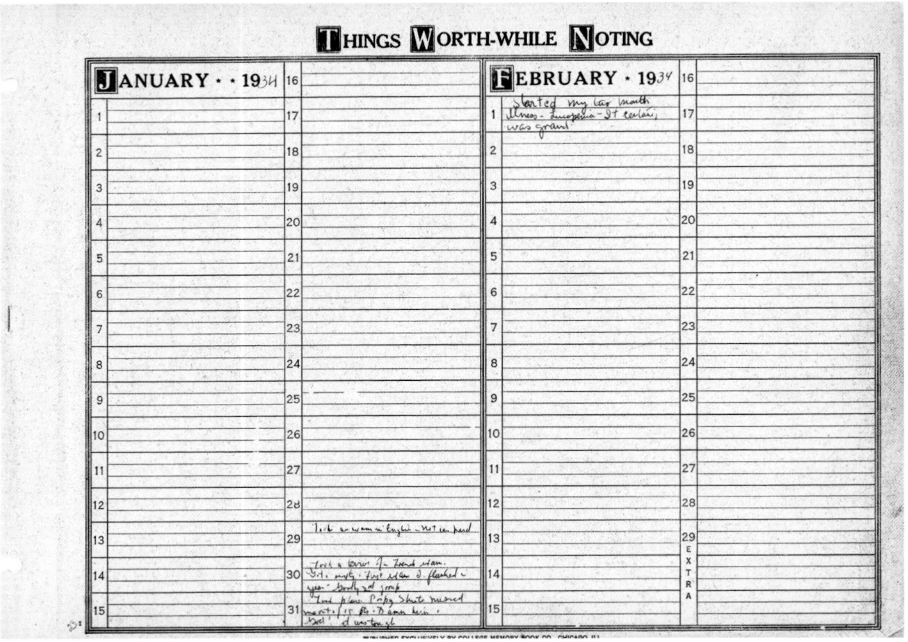

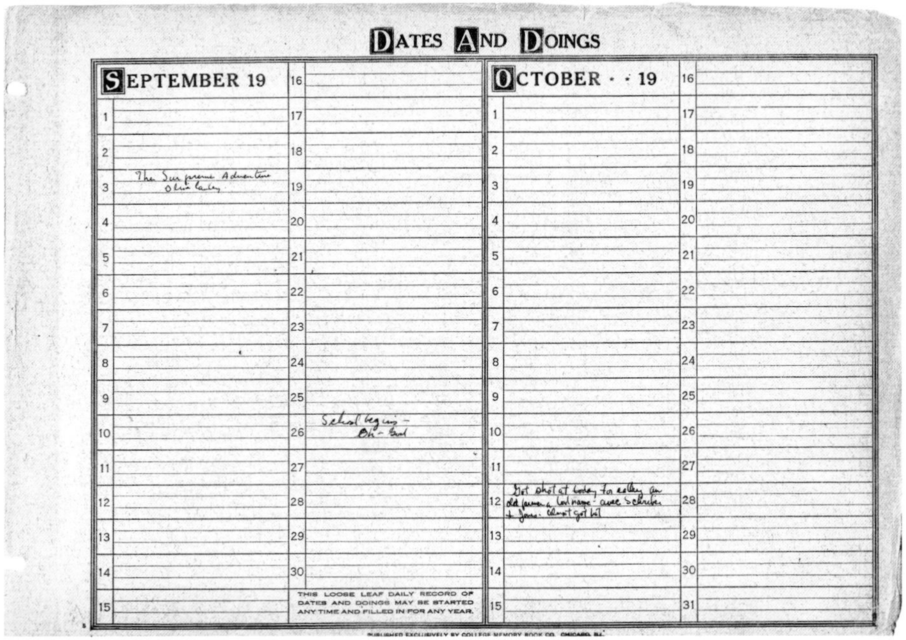

January

Took an exam in English—not very hard

Took a terror of a French exam.
Got a sixty—First exam I flunked in year—
Goodby 3rd group [*Membership in "3rd group"
required a 75% average*]

Took Plane [*geometry*] Plupie Shute missed
me out of 15 pts. Damn him.
God! it was tough
[*William George Shute, a Choate faculty
member, taught math, science, and aeronautics*]

February

Started my two month illness—Lucopenia—It
certainly was grand

The Supreme Adventure
Olive Cawley [*Jack's high school sweetheart*]

School begins—Oh God

Got shot at today for calling an old farmer a bad name—
avec Schriber & Jones. Almost got hit

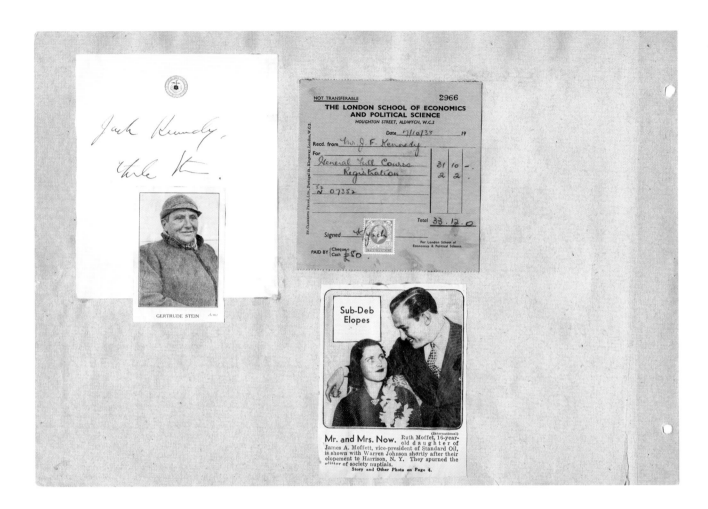

In January 1935, Gertrude Stein visited Choate to deliver a talk on writing, which Jack attended. After the talk, he asked for Stein's autograph and inserted it here along with her photograph.[12, 13]

Several items, including this receipt from the London School of Economics where JFK studied briefly after graduating from Choate, and a clipping about the 1936 elopement of his friend Ruth Moffet, were added after his Choate years.[14]

5

The Kennedy Family in London, July 4, 1938

Photograph by Dorothy Wilding

John F. Kennedy Presidential Library and Museum

Back, left to right: Joe Jr., Eunice, Patricia, Rosemary, Jack

Front, left to right: Kathleen, Bobby, Teddy, Ambassador and Mrs. Kennedy, Jean

In December 1937, Joseph P. Kennedy was appointed U.S. Ambassador to Great Britain. It was among the most prestigious of all the diplomatic posts—one he had lobbied for over many months. When he and his photogenic family arrived in London in March 1938, they were treated as celebrities and warmly welcomed into English society.

But Ambassador Kennedy's tenure soon ran into difficulty. He was profoundly averse to war and, assuming his post as Europe stood on the edge of World War II, he soon found himself increasingly at odds with the British and U.S. governments. He remained tolerant of Adolf Hitler's Nazi regime in Germany, and underestimated Britain's ability and resolve to resist the aggression of the Nazi military machine that marked the onset of World War II in Europe. Ambassador Kennedy resigned his post in the late fall of 1940.

6

John F. Kennedy's United States Navy Identification Card

John F. Kennedy Presidential Library and Museum

JFK's service in the Navy during World War II was a formative experience in his life. He actively sought combat duty and served in the Pacific Theater as commander of patrol torpedo (PT) boats 109 and 59. He emerged from his military service a decorated combat hero.

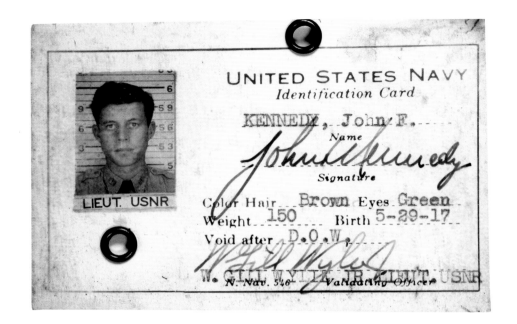

7

Lieutenant (jg) John F. Kennedy's Training Certificate from the Motor Torpedo Boat Squadrons Training Center, Melville, Rhode Island, December 1, 1942

John F. Kennedy Presidential Library and Museum

After completing Officers Training School in Chicago in September 1942, JFK volunteered for PT boat duty. While undergoing training in Rhode Island, he was promoted to lieutenant (junior grade).

Lt. (jg) John F. Kennedy aboard PT 109 in the South Pacific, 1943

John F. Kennedy Presidential Library and Museum

8

Logbook, PT 109, April 1, 1943 – June 30, 1943

Courtesy National Archives, Washington, DC

In the early morning hours of August 2, 1943, the boat was rammed and sunk by a Japanese destroyer. JFK instantly lost two of his crew and led the survivors through a harrowing ordeal that ended six days later with their rescue. He emerged from the experience with a battle-tested view of war that would come to shape his perspective as Commander-in-Chief.

As recorded here, Lieutenant (jg) John F. Kennedy took command of PT 109 on April 25, 1943. This is the last logbook for PT 109. The book that was in use in August 1943 went down with the boat.

9

PT boat lapel pin worn by JFK during World War II, and presented to his mother after the sinking of PT 109

John F. Kennedy Presidential Library and Museum

"PT 109—Apr 25, 1943—1100—Lt (jg) J.F. Kennedy assumed command of boat"

10

Logbook, PT 59, October 1, 1943— December 31, 1943

Courtesy National Archives, Washington, DC

Recovered from his injuries after the sinking of PT 109, Kennedy continued his naval service in the Solomon Islands as commander of another PT boat. In October 1943, he was promoted to lieutenant and came aboard PT 59 which, under his command, was part of a rescue mission that evacuated Marine and naval personnel from a sinking vessel near Choiseul Island. By mid-November, he was gaunt and exhausted, both mentally and physically. This page reveals that, on November 18, 1943, he was directed by a doctor to leave PT 59. On January 3, 1944, he returned to the United States, where he received further medical treatment. He was retired from the Navy on physical disability in March 1945.[15]

11

Navy Model of PT 109, displayed by President Kennedy in the Oval Office

Courtesy Naval Surface Warfare Center, Carderock Division, West Bethesda, Maryland

12

U.S. Flag from PT 109, replaced July 1943, the month before the boat was sunk

John F. Kennedy Presidential Library
and Museum

This wind-tattered flag, replaced by a new one shortly before PT 109 was sunk, is one of the few physical remnants from the boat that still exists.

13

Citation for Navy and Marine Corps Medal, presented June 12, 1944

John F. Kennedy Presidential Library and Museum

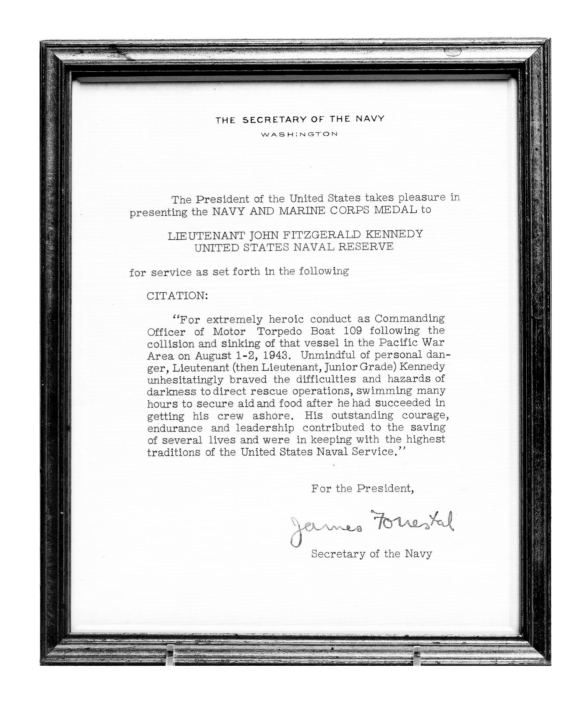

THE SECRETARY OF THE NAVY

WASHINGTON

The President of the United States takes pleasure in presenting the NAVY AND MARINE CORPS MEDAL to

LIEUTENANT JOHN FITZGERALD KENNEDY
UNITED STATES NAVAL RESERVE

for service as set forth in the following

CITATION:

"For extremely heroic conduct as Commanding Officer of Motor Torpedo Boat 109 following the collision and sinking of that vessel in the Pacific War Area on August 1-2, 1943. Unmindful of personal danger, Lieutenant (then Lieutenant, Junior Grade) Kennedy unhesitatingly braved the difficulties and hazards of darkness to direct rescue operations, swimming many hours to secure aid and food after he had succeeded in getting his crew ashore. His outstanding courage, endurance and leadership contributed to the saving of several lives and were in keeping with the highest traditions of the United States Naval Service."

For the President,

James Forrestal

Secretary of the Navy

14

John F. Kennedy's passport application, September 1951

John F. Kennedy Presidential Library and Museum

JFK returned home from the war in 1944. Following his physical recovery from back surgery, he decided to pursue a career in politics. A war hero and son of a wealthy and politically well connected Boston family, Kennedy was elected in 1946 to represent the 11th District of Massachusetts in the U.S. House of Representatives, where he served three terms. By the fall of 1951, he set his sights on a seat in the U.S. Senate. With a growing focus on and lifelong fascination with foreign affairs, he embarked on a seven-week tour of the Middle and Far East.

15

Home movies of Congressman Kennedy's trip to the Middle and Far East, October – November 1951, selection of still frames

Film footage probably shot by JFK and his siblings, Patricia and Robert, while sightseeing

John F. Kennedy Presidential Library and Museum

Representative Kennedy's tour of the Middle and Far East included visits to Israel, Iran, Pakistan, India, Singapore, Thailand, French Indochina, Korea, and Japan. Speaking to a nationwide radio audience upon his return, he said that he wanted to understand how the people in those regions viewed the United States "and what you and I might do in our respective capacities to further the cause of peace."

His brother, Robert, and sister, Patricia, seen in footage from some of the trip's lighter moments, accompanied him on the tour.[16]

16

Ministry of Health form filled out and signed by John F. Kennedy as he traveled from Israel to Iran, October 8, 1951

John F. Kennedy Presidential Library and Museum

MINISTRY OF HEALTH
PERSONAL DECLARATION OF ORIGIN AND HEALTH
(International Form)
(For passengers on aircraft)

Port of arrival: _____

1. Name in full: *Kennedy John F.*
   (Block Letters. Surname First)

2. Nationality: *American*   3. Passport number: _____

4. Permanent (home) address: *122 Bowdoin St, Boston, Mass - USA*

5. Address (in full) to which immediately proceeding:
   Teheran - Iran

   _____

   _____

6. State below the town, locality or airport where you spent the 14 nights prior to arrival in this country

   Last night: *Tel Aviv*   8 nights ago: *New York*
   2 nights ago: *enroute from Rome*   9 nights ago: *" "*
   3 nights ago: *Paris*   10 nights ago: *" "*
   4 nights ago: *Paris*   11 nights ago: *" "*
   5 nights ago: *Paris*   12 nights ago: *" "*
   6 nights ago: *New York*   13 nights ago: *" "*
   7 nights ago: *New York*   14 nights ago: *" "*

7. I am in possession of a certificate of inoculation or vaccination against—: (Answer Yes or No)
   Yellow Fever *yes*   Smallpox *yes*
   Cholera *yes*   Typhus *yes*

8. I declare that I have had no illness within the past 14 days except as follows:—

   _____

I declare that the information given above is correct to the best of my knowledge and belief.

Date *Oct 8, 1951*   Signature *John F. Kennedy*

KLM 889 - 30,000 - 651 - 95

17

JFK's radio report on his trip to the Middle and Far East, November 14, 1951, title page

John F. Kennedy Presidential Library and Museum

Representative Kennedy delivered this report by radio to a nationwide audience following his travels.

Excerpts from the radio report

"Foreign policy today . . . overshadows everything else. Expenditures, taxation, domestic prosperity, the extent of social services—all hinge on the basic issue of peace or war."

". . . Communism cannot be met effectively by merely the force of arms. It is the peoples themselves that must be led to reject it . . ."

"The true enemy of the Arab world is poverty and want . . . The central core of our Middle Eastern policy is . . . the rebirth of our traditional sympathy for . . .the desires of men to be free."

" . . . The failure of our earlier China policy and the loss of the friendship the millions of Chinese once held for us are tragedies beyond all measure. Whether we shall ever recoup these losses, no one can say. . . ."

"In Indo-China . . . the task is . . . to build strong native non-Communist sentiment . . ."

"We must . . . find real and enduring answers to these many problems. Their starting point lies in . . . the foundations of American life, its realization of the right of others to the independence that we cherish . . . its emphasis on the freedoms of the individual and its passionate belief that man can deal effectively with his enemies, such as poverty and want. The peoples of the East are wise enough to know whether our efforts are guided by such a spirit . . ."

Please return to Ted Reardon

FOR RELEASE ALL EDITIONS THURSDAY MORNING NEWSPAPERS

ADVANCE COPY

OF REPORT ON

HIS TRIP TO THE MIDDLE AND FAR EAST

BY

THE HON. JOHN F. KENNEDY

REPRESENTATIVE FROM ELEVENTH CONGRESSIONAL DISTRICT

OF MASSACHUSETTS

OVER

THE MUTUAL BROADCASTING NETWORK

FROM

STATION WOR

NEW YORK, NEW YORK

Wednesday, November 14, 1951 - 10:30 P.M.

"Foreign policy today . . . overshadows everything else."

18

JFK's travel journal, October – November 1951

John F. Kennedy Presidential Library and Museum

In the journal that he kept throughout his seven weeks of travel, JFK recorded these notes from his meeting with General Dwight D. Eisenhower, which took place in Paris where JFK had stopped en route to the Middle East. Eisenhower, who had led the Allied forces in Europe during World War II, was then serving as Supreme Allied Commander Europe (SACEUR).

Transcription

"Oct. 3—Paris—I talked with General Eisenhower Biddle & MacArthur at SHAEF Headquarters. Eisenhower looking very fit—seemed disturbed at news of last few days. Attacked those who critized [sic.] those who attacked settlements made during war. Said he was merely fighting a war. Had very little to do with them. States that he warned Truman at Potsdam not to beg Russians to come into war. Cannot understand why we gave Sakhalin Islands to Russians, however. Says that Forrestal warned him in 1944 about the Russians in Normandy. Says we must hang on to Muslim world. The trouble with us is that we expect everyone to go completely our way & we are sore if they don't. Says that King of Egypt friendly to us but our papers caricature him so that he is embittered."

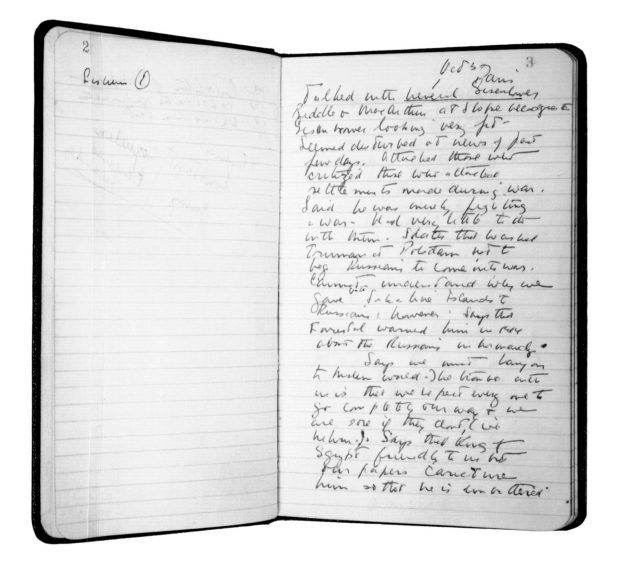

19

Invitation to the wedding of Jacqueline Lee Bouvier and Senator John Fitzgerald Kennedy, September 12, 1953

John F. Kennedy Presidential Library and Museum

Two years after Representative Kennedy met Jacqueline Bouvier, a photographer and journalist working for the *Washington Times-Herald*, they were engaged. Intelligent, artistic, and athletic, she had an adventurous spirit, a love of history and literature that she and JFK shared, and a style all her own. They married on September 12, 1953 in Newport, Rhode Island less than a year after JFK was elected Senator from Massachusetts.

20

Home movies of the wedding of John F. Kennedy and Jacqueline Bouvier, September 12, 1953, selection of still frames

Film footage shot by Paul B. "Red" Fay, Jr., friend of the groom

John F. Kennedy Presidential Library and Museum

21

Jacqueline Kennedy's wedding portrait, September 12, 1953

Photograph by Bradford Bachrach

John F. Kennedy Presidential Library and Museum
© Bachrach

22

Name plate from the desk used by John F. Kennedy in the U.S. Senate chamber

John F. Kennedy Presidential Library and Museum

23

John F. Kennedy's chair from the United States Senate Chamber

John F. Kennedy Presidential Library and Museum

Two days before JFK's inauguration, a Senate Committee voted to give the incoming President his Senate chair.

"The Senate is the most interesting job in the country."

—Senator John F. Kennedy, 1957 television interview

United States Senate Chamber, 1959
Associated Press

24

Profiles in Courage, first edition, 1956

John F. Kennedy Presidential Library and Museum

In 1954, the year after JFK began his first term as U.S. Senator, he was forced to take a leave of absence to undergo major surgery on his back. During the long period of recuperation, he indulged his love of history, writing a book about a topic that fascinated him: political courage. Titled *Profiles in Courage*, the book presents the case studies of eight Senators throughout U.S. history who suffered career-threatening consequences as a result of taking unpopular, but principled stands. Published in 1956, the book received the Pulitzer Prize in biography in 1957.

After signing a copy of his book, Senator Kennedy tosses it back to an admirer

Photograph by Paul Schutzer

The LIFE Picture Collection/Getty Images

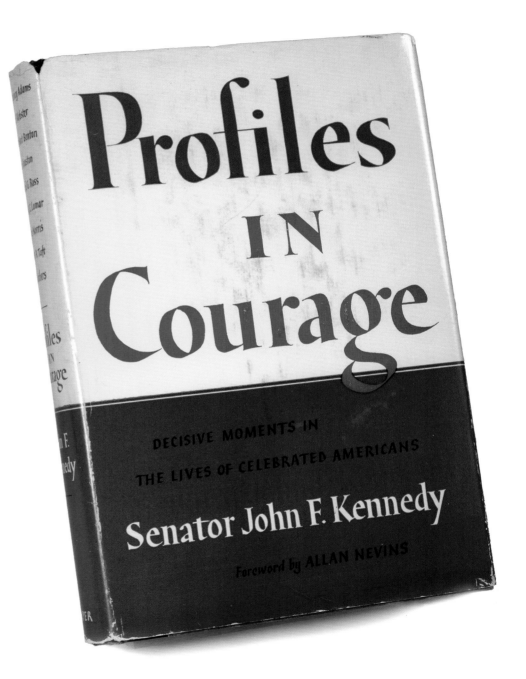

25

JFK's notes in preparation of *Profiles in Courage*

John F. Kennedy Presidential Library and Museum

The first line in these notes is an early version of the opening sentence of Chapter 1, which, in the published version reads, "This is a book about that most admirable of human virtues—courage."

Transcription

"This is a book about courage—in a more profound sense a book about the meaning and substance of political responsibility. Eight examples have been chosen. All eight were United States Senators—This does not mean of course that political courage is found only in the Senate—it is found every where that men hold office who believe that there are certain things more important. . ."

26

Draft of the preface to *Profiles in Courage*, not dated

John F. Kennedy Presidential Library and Museum

In the final published version of the book, JFK inserted the following sentence in the preface, acknowledging the contribution of Ted Sorensen who served as his legislative and administrative assistant and speechwriter: "The greatest debt is owed to my research associate Theodore C. Sorensen for his invaluable assistance in the assembly and preparation of the material upon which this book is based." JFK's draft of that sentence is shown at right.

He later bristled at allegations that the book was actually ghostwritten by Sorensen. Kennedy had assembled a team of historians to assist with the research, several of whom are mentioned in the preface. Although Sorensen provided initial drafts, he later asserted that it was JFK who conceived the book, selected the Senators to be profiled, immersed himself in the materials and then wrote or rewrote each of the chapters.

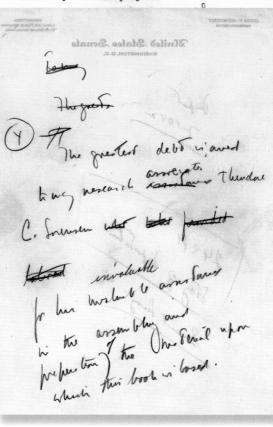

27

Letter from John F. Kennedy to his sister, Eunice Kennedy Shriver, July 26, 1955

John F. Kennedy Presidential Library and Museum

July 26, 1955

Mrs. Eunice Shriver
220 East Walton Place
Chicago, Illinois

Dear Eunice:

Would you and Sarge and your friends mull over the following suggested titles for the book and let me know as soon as possible which you think is the best:

1. Men of Courage
2. Eight were Courageous
3. Call the Roll
4. Profiles of Courage.

Sincerely,

JFK:gl

28

Book jacket design proposed for *Profiles in Courage*, showing the names of the eight Senators selected by JFK to be profiled in the book

John F. Kennedy Presidential Library and Museum

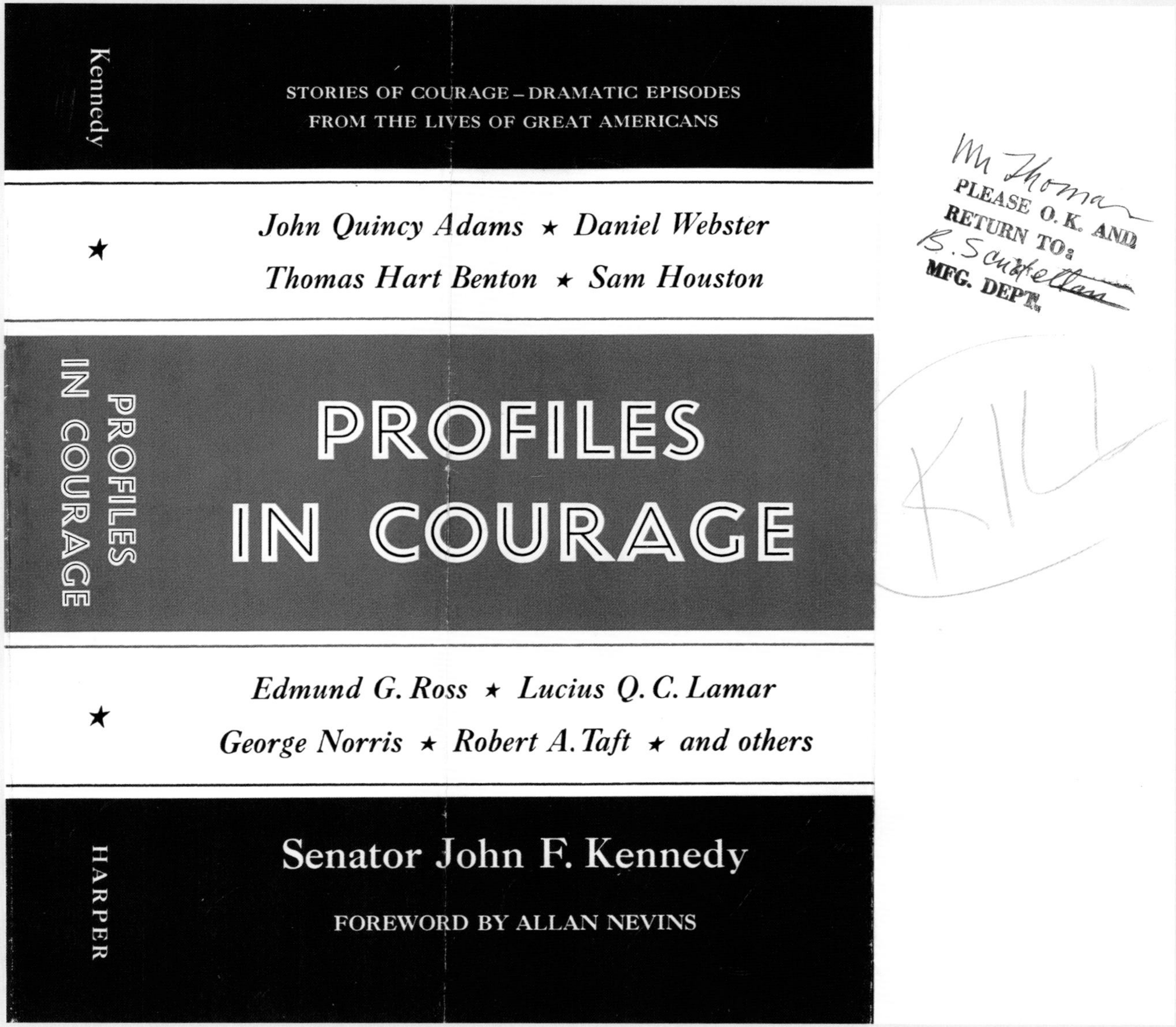

STORIES OF COURAGE – DRAMATIC EPISODES
FROM THE LIVES OF GREAT AMERICANS

Kennedy

★ *John Quincy Adams* ★ *Daniel Webster*
Thomas Hart Benton ★ *Sam Houston*

PROFILES IN COURAGE

★ *Edmund G. Ross* ★ *Lucius Q. C. Lamar*
George Norris ★ *Robert A. Taft* ★ *and others*

HARPER

Senator John F. Kennedy

FOREWORD BY ALLAN NEVINS

Portrait of Senator John F. Kennedy featured on the back cover of *Profiles in Courage*

Photograph by Hank Walker, April 1954

"For, in a democracy . . . We, the people, are the boss, and we will get the kind of political leadership, be it good or bad, that we demand and deserve."[17]

—John F. Kennedy, from the concluding chapter, *Profiles in Courage*, 1956

29

Pulitzer Prize in Letters, Biography, for "Profiles in Courage," May 6, 1957

John F. Kennedy Presidential Library and Museum

Profiles in Courage received mostly excellent reviews, remained on the bestseller list for more than a year, and sold some 2 million copies. The Pulitzer Prize added luster to Kennedy's name, established his reputation as a Senator-scholar, and fueled his rise to national prominence while he considered a run for the Presidency.

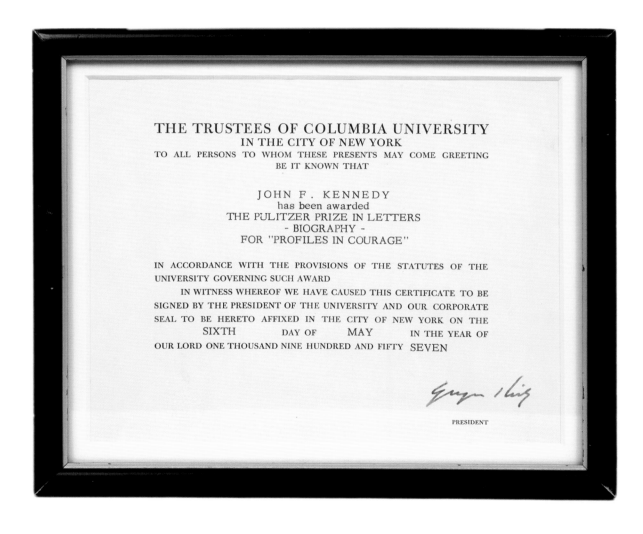

30

Television interview of Senator John F. Kennedy, conducted by Martin Agronsky for NBC's show, "Look Here," November 24, 1957, still frames from the recorded interview

John F. Kennedy Presidential Library and Museum
© NBC

JFK served in the Senate from 1953 until 1960. A November 1957 television interview covered a wide range of topics: JFK's family background and religion, the separation of Church and State, intellectualism in American politics ("Americans like brains," said Kennedy), his war injuries and general health, the state of American politics, and his book, *Profiles in Courage*. Agronsky gingerly approached the topic of JFK's Presidential aspirations, without directly posing a question. The interview's final question related to the impending birth of Senator and Mrs. Kennedy's baby. Their daughter, Caroline, was born just three days later.

Transcripts from the Interview

Agronsky: Why'd you end up in politics?

JFK: I'm descended from a long line of politicians. My grandfather was Mayor of Boston. I had a number of great-uncles who were state Senators, and my father was involved in political life. So at least the environment always at home was never really business as much as it was public affairs. So that was the natural direction – at least the subject of interest for all of us.

Could your religion conceivably ever influence your conduct or judgement as a Senator or as a member of the House or as a President of the United States?

Of course your religion has an effect on all your actions . . . of course your religious convictions influence you. . . . I swore an oath to defend the Constitution when I went in the Navy and I've taken it four times since in my elections to Congress. It's the same oath, I believe, as the President takes. . . . My faith is a personal matter. . . . my obligation would be, if I were – as somebody sworn to defend the Constitution is to uphold the Constitution. . . . what church I go to on Sunday or what dogma of the Catholic Church I believe in is a personal matter. It's really my business and whatever other faith any other American may have is their business. But it does not involve public questions of policy or as the Constitution defines the responsibilities of a President or a Senator or a member of the Armed Forces.

Senator, you've always been a kind of a literary type and cared to a considerable extent about intellectualism and intellectual problems. . . . Has the intellectual been divorced from politics in our country, or too much divorced? Insufficiently appreciated?

Of course, historically, as you know Martin, most of our early political leaders were all intellectuals . . . when you think of Hamilton and Jefferson and Adams. They would certainly rank among the top intellectuals in this country's experience – in addition to being top political leaders. As a matter of fact, in 1856 the Republicans sent three people around the campaign circuit: William Cullen Bryant, Longfellow and Emerson. All made speeches. In those days all the eggheads were Republicans. So there's been a very intimate tie – now there is some evidence that after – at the beginning of this century, the end of the nineteenth century, that that link perhaps was broken. And in this century there have been periods when there's been some suspicion of those too interested in intellectual things. So that the trend has gone up and down, but certainly in the beginning the tie was intimate. It's not perhaps intimate enough now. . . . I think Americans like brains. . . .

Senator, you're an extremely expecting expectant father at this point. I believe your first baby's due to be born on Wednesday, and I wonder if I can ask you a rather personal question. . . . If you were to have a son would you encourage a political career for him?

Yes. And I hope if I had a daughter I might encourage her to play some part. . . . I don't think that this should be confined to men only. But I would, definitely. I hope he would grow up to be, if not a politician in the sense to devoting all of his time, I would hope that whatever he did do that he would have some sense of responsibility for what went on.

31

Remarks of Senator John F. Kennedy, Yakima, Washington, June 21, 1959, selected pages

John F. Kennedy Presidential Library and Museum

In June 1959, Senator Kennedy's campaign travels brought him and his wife to Washington State. Addressing a Democratic dinner in Yakima, he quoted three U.S. Presidents, American writer Robert Sherwood, Shakespeare's King Lear, American historian Vernon Louis Parrington, U.S. Supreme Court Justice Oliver Wendell Holmes, and British statesman David Lloyd George.

While waiting to deliver the speech, he decided to close with the last lines of Alfred Lord Tennyson's poem, "Ulysses," but could not quite remember the words. So he scribbled a note to his wife, who had memorized the poem as a child: "Give me last lines from Ulysses beginning, 'Come my friends.'" Just below his note, she wrote down the rest of the poem from memory (facing page, left).

On the last page of the speech (facing page, right), near the bottom, JFK wrote, "In the poem Ulysses—by Tennyson—the poet tells us how Ulysses in his old age decides to set out once again on a last adventure."

REMARKS OF SENATOR JOHN F. KENNEDY (DEM.-MASS.) AT THE
DEMOCRATIC DINNER, YAKIMA, WASHINGTON, SUNDAY, JUNE 21, 1959

. . . I have always thought it an interesting commentary on history that all Democratic dinners across the country always link together the two founding fathers of our party, Andrew Jackson and Thomas Jefferson. For we ought to realize that neither of them was beloved by all Democrats in their day. For example, one prominent Democrat is quoted as saying, in 1824:

> "I feel much alarmed at the prospect of seeing General Jackson President. He is one of the most unfit men I know of for such a place. He has very little respect for law . . . his passions are terrible . . . he is a dangerous man."

This was the statement of Thomas Jefferson.

Ulysses The words he puts in mouth of Ulysses Here here ___

Give me last lines from Ulysses

beginning their Ulysses Ulysses

Come my friends — 'tis not too late to
seek a newer world

Sitting well in order let us smite the sounding furrow
For my purpose holds to sail beyond the sunset
And the baths of all the western Stars - until I die

It may be that the gulfs will wash us down
It may be we shall reach the Happy Isles
And see the great Achilles whom we knew —
Though we are not Now what we once were
That strength which in old days moved earth & heaven
That which we are we are —
One equal — temper of heroic hearts
Deal harshly perhaps Made weak by Time & Fate but strong in will
to strive, to seek, to find, & not to yield.

---

earth's population -- a feat not
accomplished since Cain slew Abel.

But now we have taken in our human
hands the source of energy that has lighted
the universe from the beginning of time --
we can ignite stars on earth hotter than
any that shine in the heavens -- and,
indeed, we are racing to launch our own
stars and our own moons.

To keep our faith and our freedom
alive will require leadership better
equipped than any since Jackson's day to
make clear to our people the vast spectrum
of our challenges.

Wilson — Lincoln

Conclude with the poem Ulysses — by Tennyson —
the final lines where Ulysses in his old age
decides to set out once again on a last adventure.

32

John F. Kennedy's suitcase used during the 1960 Presidential primaries and election

John F. Kennedy Presidential Library and Museum

Kennedy prepared for a Presidential run long before he made his formal announcement of candidacy. He traveled throughout the United States, acquainting himself with the voters and local Democratic Party leaders in every region. Among the challenges he faced as a candidate was an entrenched bias against Catholics and a perception that, at age 42, he was too young and inexperienced for the nation's highest office.

When he did make a formal announcement on January 2, 1960, he asserted his qualifications, citing his travels across the country, his 18 years of public service—in the military during World War II and in the Congress—and his international travels. From these experiences, he said, "I have developed an image of America as fulfilling a noble and historic role as the defender of freedom in a time of maximum peril—and of the American people as confident, courageous and persevering. It is with this image that I begin this campaign."

"In the past 40 months, I have toured every state in the Union and I have talked to Democrats in all walks of life. My candidacy is therefore based on the conviction that I can win both the nomination and the election."

—Senator John F. Kennedy, January 2, 1960, announcing his candidacy for President

Campaigning in Charleston, West Virginia, April 1960

Photograph by Jacques Lowe

© Estate of Jacques Lowe

West Virginia Primary Campaign

Religious bigotry was one of JFK's greatest adversaries in the 1960 Presidential campaign. In West Virginia, he confronted the issue head-on and defeated it. Sweeping a state in which Catholics comprised barely 5 percent of the population, Senator Kennedy proved that a Catholic candidate could win over Protestant voters.

Throughout the primary, Senator Kennedy traveled the state, witnessing first-hand the hardships of West Virginians. He shone a spotlight on their plight and detailed a national plan for economic recovery. On May 10, 1960, the people of this economically distressed, overwhelmingly Protestant, hardscrabble state in Appalachia put their trust in the elegant, young Catholic Senator who spoke in a Boston accent about a brighter future. The people of West Virginia made their mark on this candidate and helped to shape the President he would become.

33

"Food for West Virginia," speech delivered at Mount Hope, West Virginia, April 20, 1960, reading copy, selected pages

John F. Kennedy Presidential Library and Museum

In some counties of West Virginia, more than one-quarter of the population had so little income they were forced to depend on food packages distributed by the federal government for subsistence. Senator Kennedy was appalled to learn that a West Virginia family with seven children only received these monthly provisions: five bags of flour, four cans of powdered eggs, three five-pound bags of cornmeal, eight pounds of shortening, four pounds of rice, and powdered milk.

Nine months after delivering this speech—on his first full day in office—President Kennedy signed an Executive Order to increase food allotments for the poor. It was his first official act as President.[18]

REMARKS OF SENATOR JOHN F. KENNEDY (DEM.-MASS.)
MOUNT HOPE, WEST VIRGINIA
WEDNESDAY MORNING, APRIL 20, 1960

COPY

FOOD FOR WEST VIRGINIA

I want to talk with you today about the most fundamental subject in life -- food.

Most of the nation takes food for granted. When I spoke recently about the millions of Americans who go to bed hungry each night, my speech was criticized by the Wall Street Journal. Impossible, they said. Not in America. Not with all our prosperity and all our food surpluses and all our welfare programs.

But the Wall Street Journal ought to come to West Virginia, to this county and to other counties like it. Because people are hungry here -- prosperity has passed them by -- food surpluses are rotting in

COPY

warehouses -- and welfare programs are not enough.

There are some surplus foods distributed by the Department of Agriculture. Some four million Americans depend on that food -- but what kind of food is it? Flour, rice and corn-meal -- sometimes some butter, cheese and dry skim milk -- and more flour, rice and corn-meal. Perhaps they'll soon be receiving lard -- sometimes there is a small amount of dry egg solid or dried beans -- but it is mostly flour, rice and corn-meal.

That diet is not the basis of a decent existence -- a healthful home -- a hopeful outlook for the child in school, the father seeking work, the mother at home. That diet

COPY

can lead only to malnutrition, chronic disease and physical handicaps. That diet is the cause of rotten teeth and shattered hopes. That diet is a disgrace in a country that calls itself the land of opportunity, the richest country on earth, the arsenal of the Free World.

I believe in helping our friends abroad -- but I also believe we must help our own here at home. In recent years Secretary Benson has sent overseas, under our surplus food disposal program, beef, chickens, turkeys, ducks, pork, sausage, potatoes, milk, orange juice, peaches, cherries and other fruits and vegetables. He has not sent only flour, rice and corn-meal. He has not expected our friends

34

"From the Coal Mines of West Virginia, Products Made from Coal"

John F. Kennedy Presidential Library and Museum

A class of sixth graders from the Meadows School in Huntington, West Virginia made this souvenir for Senator Kennedy.

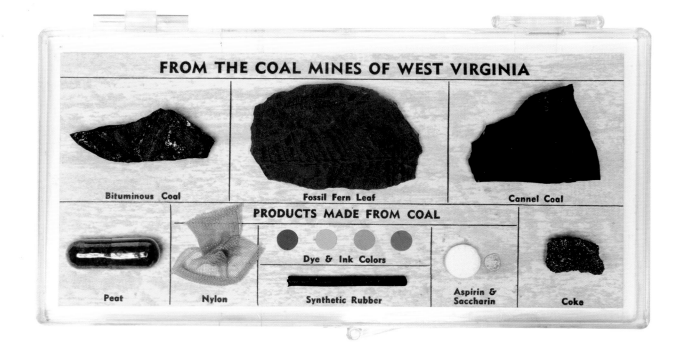

FROM THE COAL MINES OF WEST VIRGINIA

Bituminous Coal

Fossil Fern Leaf

Cannel Coal

PRODUCTS MADE FROM COAL

Dye & Ink Colors

Peat

Nylon

Synthetic Rubber

Aspirin & Saccharin

Coke

Senator John F. Kennedy campaigning in West Virginia, April 1960

Photograph by Jacques Lowe

John F. Kennedy Presidential Library and Museum
© Estate of Jacques Lowe

"While traveling from Parkersburg to Charleston, West Virginia, Kennedy spotted this group of grade-school children with their teacher. He stopped the car and climbed on top of a tractor to address the group. It seemed a desperate search for votes, since there was only one to be had, the Teacher's."

—Photographer Jacques Lowe, 1993

35

Letter from Eleanor Roosevelt to Lawrence Fuchs, December 11, 1958

John F. Kennedy Presidential Library and Museum

Like many liberal Democrats, former First Lady Eleanor Roosevelt—an influential figure inside the Democratic Party—believed that Senator Kennedy was not sufficiently liberal in his positions, particularly in the areas of civil rights and labor unions. In addition, Mrs. Roosevelt had publicly criticized JFK[19] for being slow to speak out against Joseph McCarthy, the Senator from Wisconsin who had aggressively investigated and accused many government servants of being Communist sympathizers. In 1954, the U.S. Senate censured McCarthy for conduct unbecoming a Senator. Kennedy was absent and did not vote on the resolution.

Dr. Lawrence Fuchs, who taught at Brandeis University, was an adviser to JFK, and had once co-taught a course with Mrs. Roosevelt. When JFK was seeking her support as he prepared to run for President, Professor Fuchs wrote to the former First Lady trying to arrange for her to meet with JFK. In this letter she politely declines the opportunity and expresses her admiration for another Presidential hopeful: Adlai Stevenson.

MRS. FRANKLIN D. ROOSEVELT
202 FIFTY-SIXTH STREET WEST
NEW YORK 19, N. Y.

December 11, 1958

Dear Mr. Fuchs:

Thank you so very much for your kind letter.

I would of course be glad to have dinner with you but a free date for all of us may be difficult to find.

I have met the Senator alone and socially and he is charming but greatness I have as yet not found except in Adlai.

Very sincerely yours,

Eleanor Roosevelt

36

Senator John F. Kennedy with Eleanor Roosevelt at her cottage, Val-Kill, in Hyde Park, New York, August 14, 1960

Photograph by Dr. A. David Gurewitsch

John F. Kennedy Presidential Library and Museum

One month after winning the Democratic nomination for President, JFK traveled to Hyde Park for a private luncheon with Mrs. Roosevelt, hoping to win her over. This photograph was taken moments after she agreed to fully support his candidacy. She later issued the following statement:

"John F. Kennedy came to visit me at Hyde Park. We talked together and I learned that he was truly interested in carrying on many of the things which my husband had just begun. Mr. Kennedy is a strong and determined person, who, as president, will provide the leadership for greater social security benefits which the social welfare of a civilized nation demands. I urge you to study Mr. Kennedy's programs to look at his very remarkable record in Congress, and I think you will join me in voting for John F. Kennedy for president."

— Eleanor Roosevelt, August 1960[20]

37

The Case of Martin Luther King, "blue bomb" pamphlet, November 1960

John F. Kennedy Presidential Library and Museum

Throughout the Presidential campaign, Senator Kennedy carefully steered his campaign between competing factions within the Democratic Party which stood on opposite sides of the debate over civil rights. While he expressed support for redressing racial inequality, he was concerned about losing the support of the southern Democrats who steadfastly opposed the civil rights plank in the party platform. Throughout the campaign, many African Americans remained skeptical about Kennedy's commitment to civil rights. But as an episode unfolded in the final weeks of the campaign, he won their confidence—and their votes—which proved to be critical in his razor-thin victory.

In the final days of the race, JFK's campaign printed some 3 million[21] of these pamphlets, publicizing the endorsements of Martin Luther King, Jr., his father, Martin Luther King, Sr., an influential Baptist minister, and other civil rights activists. (Senator Kennedy and his campaign had expressed support and been instrumental in King's release following his arrest for taking part in a peaceful protest of a whites-only restaurant in Atlanta, Georgia.) On the Sunday before Election Day, the pamphlets were distributed in African American churches across the country. The pamphlet came to be known as the "blue bomb" for its enormous impact on public opinion. Throughout the episode, the Republican candidate, Vice President Richard Nixon, also contemplated whether to respond and chose to remain silent regarding King's plight.

On Election Day, the endorsements carried in this pamphlet may well have tipped the balance in Kennedy's favor in the battleground states.

"I never intend to reject a man running for President of the United States just because he is a Catholic. Religious bigotry is as immoral, un-democratic, un-American and un-Christian as racial bigotry."

–Martin Luther King, Jr.

Martin Luther King, Jr., shortly after he was arrested for protesting the whites-only policy of an Atlanta restaurant, October 19, 1960

Associated Press

The dozens of protesters arrested with Martin Luther King, Jr. on October 19, 1960, at the Atlanta restaurant were soon released. But King was held on the basis of a minor traffic violation, for which he was sentenced to four months of hard labor on a road gang, and transferred in the middle of the night from Atlanta to a remote rural prison. Terrified for her husband's life, Coretta Scott King, contacted a Kennedy associate.

JFK and his campaign manager, Robert F. Kennedy, were concerned about alienating white Southern Democrats who opposed the civil rights movement. However, Senator Kennedy reached out to Mrs. King, who was then pregnant with the couple's second child. In a telephone call later widely publicized, he expressed his concern for her husband and offered to assist. Meanwhile, Robert Kennedy contacted the sentencing judge and managed to secure King's release on October 27, 1960.

38

Telegram from President Dwight D. Eisenhower to President-elect John F. Kennedy, November 9, 1960

John F. Kennedy Presidential Library and Museum

President Eisenhower greets President-elect Kennedy as he arrives at the White House for a meeting, December 6, 1960

Associated Press

```
                                    Telegram from Augusta 4:37 PM
President Elect John F. Kennedy
Hyannis Port, Massachusetts

               I REFER TO MY ORIGINAL TELEGRAM
TO YOU    SENT    A FEW HOURS AGO.  I WOULD LIKE YOU TO KNOW
THAT I STAND READY TO MEET WITH YOU AT ANY MUTUALLY AGREEABLE
TIME TO CONSIDER PROBLEMS OF CONTINUITY OF GOVERNMENT AND
ORDERLY TRANSFER OF EXECUTIVE RESPONSIBILITIES ON JANUARY 20TH
FROM MY ADMINISTRATION TO YOURS.
               IN THE MEANTIME OR EVEN IN LIEU
THERE OF, IN ORDER TO FACILITATE AND PREPARE FOR THIS TRANSFER
I WOULD BE HAPPY TO HAVE ONE OF YOUR ASSISTANTS MEET WITH
MY PRINCIPAL STAFF ASSISTANT, WILTON B. PERSONS TO WHOM I AM
```

```
                           2
ASSIGNING COORDINATING RESPONSIBILITY.  I WILL BE PREPARED TO
MAKE ARRANGEMENTS BY WHICH REPRESENTATIVES DESIGNATED BY YOU
                         PRINCIPAL
COULD MEET WITH THE    /         HEADS OF THE EXECUTIVE DEPARTMENTS
MEETINGS OF THIS KIND OVER THE COMING WEEKS WITH THE DIRECTOR
OF THE BUREAU OF THE BUDGET MIGHT FOR EXAMPLE BE IMPORTANT IN
PROVIDING INFORMATION TO YOU CONCERNING THE XXX BUDGET NOW IN
PREPARATION.  IN ADDITION, THE SECRETARY OF STATE WILL BE
PREPARED FOR MEETINGS TO PROVIDE INFORMATION ON FOREIGN POLICY
ACTIVITIES ON WHICH THERE WILL BE SPECIAL NEED FOR CONTINUITY
UNTIL YOU SHALL HAVE HAD OPPORTUNITY AFTER INAUGURATION TO
ARRANGE THESE MATTERS TO YOUR SATISFACTION.
                              DWIGHT D. EISENHOWER
```

39, 40

Top hat and brown suede gloves, worn by President Kennedy to his inauguration

John F. Kennedy Presidential Library and Museum

John F. Kennedy became the 35th President of the United States on January 20, 1961, delivering one of the most enduring inaugural addresses in the nation's history.

President-elect and Mrs. Kennedy depart their Georgetown home on Inauguration Day, January 20, 1961

Getty/Bettman

41

Inauguration ceremonies program, January 20, 1961

John F. Kennedy Presidential Library and Museum

President Kennedy's inaugural ceremony was the first to include a poet on the program.

Invited to participate in the official ceremony, Robert Frost, the preeminent American poet, composed a poem, "Dedication," for the occasion. Unable to read the text of the new poem in the bright sunlight, he instead recited his poem, "The Gift Outright," from memory.

*"A Golden Age of Poetry and Power
Of which this noonday's the beginning hour."*

—From "Dedication," a poem written by Robert Frost for the inaugural ceremony

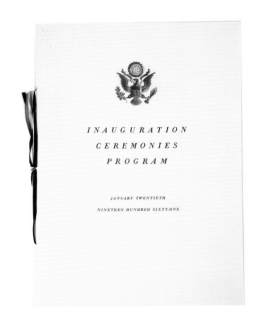

INAUGURATION
CEREMONIES
PROGRAM

JANUARY TWENTIETH
NINETEEN HUNDRED SIXTY-ONE

Program

Selection by the United States Marine Band.

Invocation by His Eminence Richard Cardinal Cushing.

Solo by Miss Marian Anderson.

Prayer by His Eminence Archbishop Iakovos.

The oath of office will be administered to the Vice President by the Honorable Sam Rayburn.

Prayer by The Reverend Dr. John Barclay.

Poem by Mr. Robert Frost.

The oath of office will be administered to the President by the Chief Justice of the United States.

Inaugural Address by the President of the United States.

Benediction by Rabbi Dr. Nelson Glueck.

The Star-Spangled Banner by the United States Marine Band.

42

Draft of Ernest Hemingway's tribute to President Kennedy, penned after watching the inaugural address on television, January 1961

John F. Kennedy Presidential Library and Museum

Ernest Hemingway was one of the many writers, artists, and poets invited to the inauguration. Unable to attend due to illness, Hemingway watched the ceremony on television, like 60 million of his fellow citizens. He later handwrote a tribute which he sent to a friend of the Kennedys who was compiling a scrapbook of congratulatory messages as a memento for the President.

Shown here is a draft. The final message, in its entirety reads as follows:

"Watching the inauguration from Rochester there was the happiness and the hope and the pride and how beautiful we thought Mrs. Kennedy was and then how deeply moving the inaugural address was. Watching on the screen I was sure our President would stand any of the heat to come as he had taken the cold of that day. Each day since I have renewed my faith and tried to understand the practical difficulties of governing he must face as they arise and admire the true courage he brings to them. It is a good thing to have a brave man as our President in times as tough as these are for our country and the world."

43

Presidential Seal from the lectern at the Department of State, where President Kennedy conducted his televised press conferences

John F. Kennedy Presidential Library and Museum

The Presidency

As a candidate running for office in the midst of the Cold War, John F. Kennedy had campaigned hard on the issue of American strength. The power and prestige of the United States was slipping, he had warned, and shoring up America's military, economic, technological, and moral foundations would be the best defense for the nation and for the cause of freedom around the world. Beginning January 20, 1961, and throughout his administration, he would confront the hard issues of the day. Abroad, he considered among the major issues of his time to be the communist threat, a nuclear arms race that threatened the world's very existence, turmoil in newly independent African states, conflict in the former French colonies of Southeast Asia, and the security of Western Europe. At home his focus would be on economic growth, racial unrest, technological advancement, and anti-poverty programs.

"During my years in the Senate I have come to understand that the Presidency is the ultimate source of action. The Senate is not."

—Senator John F. Kennedy, Fall 1960[22]

44

President Kennedy's notes from his first full day as President, January 21, 1961

John F. Kennedy Presidential Library and Museum

These notes reveal that one of the first orders of business was to plan a meeting with the nation's legislative leaders. Evelyn Lincoln, the President's personal secretary, annotated the President's notes at the top of the page. The notes at the bottom of the page were made by Kenneth O'Donnell, the President's White House appointments secretary.

45

Portrait of Senator John F. Kennedy, 1959

Photograph by Fabian Bachrach

John F. Kennedy Presidential Library and Museum
© Bachrach

This photograph, selected to be the official Presidential portrait, was actually taken before Kennedy was President. During a 10-minute photo session that was squeezed into then-Senator Kennedy's busy schedule at the Capitol, the photographer snapped six images. He later recalled, "I had to work fast. He doesn't sit still very long."[23]

The image was later displayed in federal buildings and circulated to the general public as the President's official portrait throughout the years of the Kennedy administration.

46

Stamp with the Presidential Seal, traditionally used for correspondence with the Congress, displayed by President Kennedy in the Oval Office

John F. Kennedy Presidential Library and Museum

Senator John F. Kennedy at a press event, Omaha, Nebraska, August 1959

Photograph by Jacques Lowe

© Estate of Jacques Lowe

47

Viet Cong flag captured in March 1962 by members of the South Vietnamese Self Defense Corps, and later presented to President Kennedy

John F. Kennedy Presidential Library and Museum

At the end of the French Indochina War, Vietnam was temporarily partitioned under the Geneva Accord of 1954. By 1961, that agreement had crumbled and a war between the Communist-dominated North and western-allied South Vietnam was underway. A Communist insurgency had also begun *within* South Vietnam.

To prevent all of Vietnam from falling under Communist control, the Eisenhower administration had sent economic and military aid, including 700 military personnel to assist the government of South Vietnam. Over the course of his Presidency, President Kennedy gradually increased the number of American military advisers to 16,000. He also pressed the South Vietnamese government of President Ngo Dinh Diem, whose government was weakened by public protest and internal corruption, to institute political and economic reforms that were long overdue. The instability of Diem's government and its apparent ineffectiveness frustrated the United States. On November 1, 1963, in a military coup approved by the Kennedy administration, the South Vietnamese government was overthrown and President Diem was assassinated.

On the night of March 16, 1962, a South Vietnamese Self Defense Corps near the village of Trung Lap repelled an attack by the North Vietnamese Communist forces and captured this Viet Cong flag.

"This flag was captured by members of the Self Defense Corps . . . and the incident shows that they are ready to defend themselves when we give them the means."

—Roger Hilsman, Director of Intelligence and Research, Department of State, to President Kennedy

48

Map sent by Roger Hilsman, State Department, to President Kennedy to illustrate the story of the captured Viet Cong flag

John F. Kennedy Presidential Library and Museum

Responding to President Kennedy's request for the story behind the captured Viet Cong flag, the State Department's Roger Hilsman sent a letter of explanation and this map showing the village of Trung Lap, near the site where a South Vietnamese Self Defense Corps repelled an attack by the North Vietnamese Communist forces.

In his letter to the President, Hilsman explained that, on March 17, 1962, the day after the attack, a U.S. Army pilot flew the district chief from the village of Trung Lap to the site where the attack had occurred; the helicopter was fired upon twice during the short trip. Upon landing, the district chief was presented with the flag by the commander of the Self Defense Corps that had repelled the Communist attack the previous night. The district chief then showed his gratitude to the American pilot by turning the flag over to him. That American pilot, Lieutenant Colonel John R. Stockton, later asked Roger Hilsman to present the flag to President Kennedy "with the best wishes of the American helicopter pilots in Vietnam."

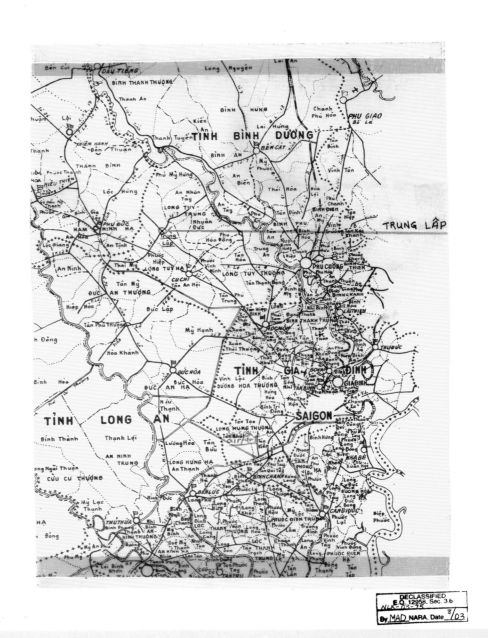

49

President Kennedy's reading copy of his address before the American Society of Newspaper Editors on the failed Bay of Pigs invasion, April 20, 1961, selected pages

John F. Kennedy Presidential Library and Museum

The Bay of Pigs invasion was the failed attempt by U.S.-backed Cuban exiles to overthrow the government of Fidel Castro. On April 17, 1961, a 1,400-man invasion force of anti-Castro Cuban exiles, Brigade 2506, landed at the Bay of Pigs beach on the south coast of Cuba. Quickly overwhelmed by a counterattack of Castro's armed forces, the invasion force was crushed two days later. More than 100 men were killed, and nearly 1,100 were taken prisoner and held in Cuba for nearly two years. Instead of toppling the Castro regime, the invasion strengthened Castro's image with the Cuban people, solidified his alignment with the Soviet Union, and emboldened Premier Nikita Khrushchev in his belief that Kennedy was weak and inexperienced.

Publicly, President Kennedy took responsibility for the invasion's failure. "We intend to profit from this lesson," he said in this address. Privately, he wondered aloud to a close adviser, "How could I have been so far off base? . . . All my life I've known better than to depend on the experts. How could I have been so stupid, to let them go ahead?"[24]

The President of a great democracy such as ours, and the editors of great newspapers such as yours, owe a common obligation to the people: an obligation to present the facts, to present them with candor, and to present them in perspective. It is with that obligation in mind that I have decided in the last 24 hours to discuss briefly at this time the recent events in Cuba.

On that unhappy island, as in so many other arenas of the contest for freedom, the news has grown worse instead of better. I have emphasized before that this was a struggle of <u>Cuban</u> patriots against a <u>Cuban</u> dictator. While we could not be expected to hide our

12

or this Administration. No other challenge is more deserving of our every effort and energy. Too long we have fixed our eyes on traditional military needs, on armies prepared to cross borders or missiles poised for flight. Now it should be clear that this is no longer enough -- that our security may be lost without the firing of a single missile or the crossing of a single border.

We intend to profit from this lesson. We intend to reexamine and reorient our forces, our tactics and our institutions. We intend to intensify our efforts for a struggle in many ways more difficult than war.

For I am convinced that we possess all the necessary resources, and all the skill, and all the added

"We intend to profit from this lesson..."

50

Department of Defense Briefing Board No. 13, February 6, 1963, showing vast areas of the western hemisphere within range of the Soviet nuclear missile sites in Cuba

John F. Kennedy Presidential Library and Museum

In the fall of 1962, the Soviet Union, under orders from Premier Nikita S. Khrushchev, began to secretly deploy a nuclear strike force in Cuba, just 90 miles from the United States, with missiles that could reach many major U.S. cities in less than five minutes. President Kennedy viewed the construction of these missile sites as intolerable, and insisted on their removal. Khrushchev refused—initially. The ensuing standoff nearly caused a nuclear exchange and is remembered in the United States as the Cuban Missile Crisis.

On October 28, 1962, as the world's mightiest military forces stood poised for warfare, Khrushchev relented. In secret negotiations Kennedy and Khrushchev had reached an agreement. After receiving secret assurances that the United States would remove its missiles from Turkey, Khrushchev announced that the Soviet missile sites in Cuba would be dismantled immediately. The peaceful resolution of the Cuban Missile Crisis was one of President Kennedy's greatest diplomatic achievements.

Three months after the crisis was resolved, the Department of Defense conducted a televised press briefing chronicling the Soviet Union's build-up and subsequent removal of nuclear weapons from Cuba. This board was used during that briefing to illustrate the gravity of the threat—nearly the entire United States was within range of the missiles.

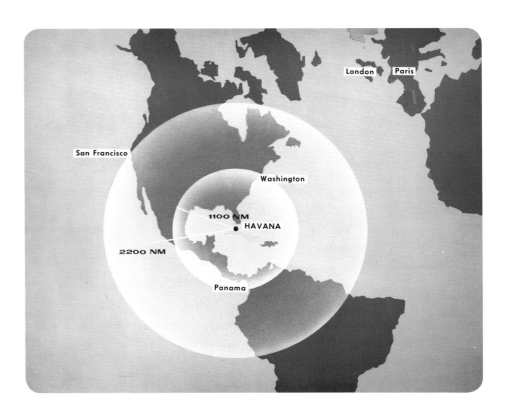

51

Cold War garden gnomes portraying President Kennedy and Premier Khrushchev

John F. Kennedy Presidential Library and Museum

A set of six garden gnomes—each one a caricature of a Cold War leader—was a gift to President Kennedy from a citizen of West Germany. In addition to the two figures shown here, the set also represented West German Chancellor Konrad Adenauer, Vice Chancellor Ludwig Erhard, West Berlin Mayor Willy Brandt, and French President Charles de Galle.

The Khrushchev figure wears only one shoe, a humorous reference to the 1960 incident at the United Nations General Assembly, when the Soviet Premier reacted in anger to a speech by removing one of his shoes and brandishing it in the air while addressing the international body.

52

Color-tinted photograph of President Kennedy and Soviet Premier Khrushchev at the Soviet Embassy in Vienna, Austria, June 4, 1961

John F. Kennedy Presidential Library and Museum

The only time President Kennedy and Soviet Premier Khrushchev met face-to-face was the summit meeting held in Vienna, Austria, June 3—4, 1961. The two leaders conversed one-on-one with only interpreters present. The talks were tough and contentious, covering a range of topics—strategic and ideological. Neither the United States nor the Soviet Union was willing to yield on the major issues that divided the two superpowers, most notably the divided city of Berlin, and no immediate progress was made in the easing of Cold War tensions. Premier Khrushchev's combative posture took President Kennedy by surprise. At the end of the summit, JFK told a reporter that the meeting was "the roughest thing in my life," and that Khrushchev "just beat the hell out of me."[25]

This photograph, inscribed in Russian by Premier Khrushchev, was later presented to President Kennedy as a gift. Translated into English, the inscription reads: "To President Kennedy/To the memory of a meeting in Vienna/November 9, 1961/N. Khrushchev."

53

President Kennedy's Cabinet Room armchair

John F. Kennedy Presidential Library and Museum

The room where the President meets with his cabinet secretaries and advisers adjoins the Oval Office. By tradition, the President's chair, is positioned at the center of the table, and the back of his chair is two inches taller than those of the cabinet secretaries.

President Kennedy meets with the Joint Chiefs of Staff in the Cabinet Room, January 25, 1961

Photograph by Jacques Lowe

© Estate of Jacques Lowe

54

Astronaut John Glenn's Historic Flight, February 20, 1962, still frames selected from NASA film footage

Courtesy NASA

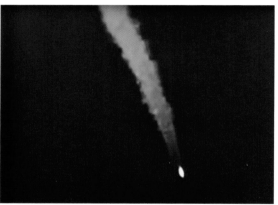

55

Umbilical Disconnect—Last Link Between Earth and John H. Glenn, Jr.'s Atlas Booster at Liftoff, February 20, 1962

John F. Kennedy Presidential Library and Museum

On April 12, 1961, Soviet cosmonaut Yuri Gagarin became the first human to go into space, orbiting the earth in a mission that lasted 108 minutes.

Alan Shepard was the first American in space, completing a suborbital flight aboard the *Freedom 7* space capsule on May 5, 1961. Nine months later, on February 20, 1962, when John Glenn orbited the earth three times piloting the *Friendship 7* space capsule, the United States took a significant step toward overtaking the Soviet Union in the race for space.

56

Project Mercury hard hat presented to President Kennedy by John Glenn on February 23, 1962

John F. Kennedy Presidential Library and Museum

Three days after Glenn's successful flight, President Kennedy visited Cape Canaveral, where he viewed the *Friendship 7* capsule and presented NASA's Distinguished Service Award to astronaut John Glenn and to Robert Gilruth, head of Project Mercury, NASA's first manned spaceflight program.

Glenn later recalled the President's curiosity and keen interest in knowing the details of the flight: "what I saw, what things looked like, how I felt during reentry, was it hot or wasn't it hot, how did I feel when it banged down on the water . . . how did it feel and what did I think about at various times."[26]

John Glenn presents the special NASA hard hat to President Kennedy, February 23, 1962

Photograph by Dean Conger

Getty Images/Corbis Historical Collection

President Kennedy's notes made in preparation of his Report to the Nation on Civil Rights

John F. Kennedy Presidential Library and Museum

In June 1963, the University of Alabama remained segregated, despite a federal court order that had mandated its desegregation. Alabama's segregationist governor, George Wallace, was defiant and promised to prevent personally, if necessary, the enrollment of two African American students in the summer session. President Kennedy and Attorney General Robert Kennedy devised a strategy to ensure the students' enrollment while avoiding the bloodshed that had ensued when the University of Mississippi was integrated the previous fall. The President insisted that the court order be upheld and federalized the Alabama National Guard to ensure the peaceful integration of the University of Alabama.

On June 11, there was a dramatic confrontation at the Tuscaloosa campus as Governor Wallace made good on his pledge to "stand in the schoolhouse door." Eventually he stepped aside when confronted by National Guardsmen, federal marshals, and Deputy Attorney General Nicholas Katzenbach. The two African American students quietly took their place on campus. To the surprise of the President's aides—and against the advice of all of them except the Attorney General—JFK decided to address the nation that very evening. The hastily-drafted speech—the last portion of which was delivered extemporaneously—is remembered as one of the high points in Kennedy's Presidency, as well as a milestone in the modern civil rights movement. For the first time a U.S. President explicitly condemned segregation as a moral wrong, and called upon Americans to join him in addressing the "moral crisis" that faced the nation by supporting his efforts to advance sweeping civil rights legislation.

Lesson
Committed to uphold

system of law

Pres. Gov.

National problem.

people getting along
w. one another

Negroes

Vivian Malone
James Hood

Fed. District Court

June 5

Vivian Malone and James Hood register for classes at the University of Alabama, June 11, 1963

OFF/AFP/Getty Images

Although President Kennedy did not name the two students in his speech, their names appear in his notes.

Vivian Malone graduated from the University of Alabama in 1965.

James Hood withdrew from the university that August and completed his undergraduate degree elsewhere. More than 30 years later, he returned to the University of Alabama where he received a doctorate in interdisciplinary studies.[27]

58

Draft of President Kennedy's Report to the American People on Civil Rights, June 11, 1963, first page

John F. Kennedy Presidential Library and Museum

Special Assistant Theodore ("Ted") C. Sorensen, whose initials appear at the top of page one, submitted this draft to the President. Writing in pencil, JFK inserted the line, "I wish to commend the students."

Excerpts from President Kennedy's televised Report to the Nation on Civil Rights, as delivered June 11, 1963

"This afternoon, following a series of threats and defiant statements, the presence of Alabama National Guardsmen was required on the University of Alabama to carry out the final and unequivocal order of the United States District Court of the Northern District of Alabama. That order called for the admission of two clearly qualified young Alabama residents who happened to have been born Negro. . . .

I hope that every American, regardless of where he lives, will stop and examine his conscience about this and other related incidents. This Nation was founded by men of many nations and backgrounds. It was founded on the principle that all men are created equal, and that the rights of every man are diminished when the rights of one man are threatened.

TCS - 2nd Draft
6/11/63

Good evening, my fellow Americans:

This afternoon, following a series of threats and defiant statements, the presence of Alabama National Guardsmen was required on the University of Alabama campus to carry out the final and unequivocal order of the United State District Court for the Northern District of Alabama. That order called for the admission of two clearly-qualified young Alabama residents who happened to have been born Negro. *I wish to Commend the students*

I hope that every American, regardless of where he lives, will stop and examine his conscience about these and related events. This nation was founded by men of many nations and backgrounds. It was founded on the principle that all men are created equal -- and that the rights of every man are diminished when the rights of one are threatened. Today we are committed to a world-wide struggle to protect and promote the rights of all who wish to be free. And when Americans are sent to Vietnam or West Berlin, to risk their lives for yours and mine, we do not ask for whites only.

It ought to be possible, therefore, for American students of any color to attend any public educational institution they select without having to be backed up by troops. It ought to be possible for American consumers of any color to receive equal service in places of public accommodation -- such as hotels, restaurants, theatres and retail stores -- without having

Today we are committed to a worldwide struggle to promote and protect the rights of all who wish to be free. And when Americans are sent to Viet-Nam or West Berlin, we do not ask for whites only. It ought to be possible, therefore, for American students of any color to attend any public institution they select without having to be backed up by troops. . . .

This is not a sectional issue. Difficulties over segregation and discrimination exist in every city, in every State of the Union, producing in many cities a rising tide of discontent that threatens the public safety. Nor is this a partisan issue. In a time of domestic crisis men of good will and generosity should be able to unite regardless of party or politics. This is not even a legal or legislative issue alone. It is better to settle these matters in the courts than on the streets, and new laws are needed at every level, but law alone cannot make men see right.

We are confronted primarily with a moral issue. It is as old as the scriptures and is as clear as the American Constitution.

The heart of the question is whether all Americans are to be afforded equal rights and equal opportunities, whether we are going to treat our fellow Americans as we want to be treated. . . .

One hundred years of delay have passed since President Lincoln freed the slaves, yet their heirs, their grandsons, are not fully free. They are not yet freed from the bonds of injustice. They are not yet freed from social and economic oppression. And this Nation, for all its hopes and all its boasts, will not be fully free until all its citizens are free.
We preach freedom around the world, and we mean it, and we cherish our freedom here at home, but are we to say to the world, and much more importantly, to each other that this is the land of the free except for the Negroes; that we have no second-class citizens except Negroes; that we have no class or caste system, no ghettoes, no master race except with respect to Negroes?

Now the time has come for this Nation to fulfill its promise. The events in Birmingham and elsewhere have so increased the cries for equality that no city or State or legislative body can prudently choose to ignore them.

The fires of frustration and discord are burning in every city, North and South, where legal remedies are not at hand. Redress is sought in the streets, in demonstrations, parades, and protests which create tensions and threaten violence and threaten lives.

We face, therefore, a moral crisis as a country and as a people. It cannot be met by repressive police action. It cannot be left to increased demonstrations in the streets. It cannot be quieted by token moves or talk. It is time to act in the Congress, in your State and local legislative body and, above all, in all of our daily lives. . . .

This is one country. It has become one country because all of us and all the people who came here had an equal chance to develop their talents. . . .

As I have said before, not every child has an equal talent or an equal ability or an equal motivation, but they should have the equal right to develop their talent and their ability and their motivation, to make something of themselves.

We have a right to expect that the Negro community will be responsible, will uphold the law, but they have a right to expect that the law will be fair, that the Constitution will be color blind, as Justice Harlan said at the turn of the century.

This is what we are talking about and this is a matter which concerns this country and what it stands for, and in meeting it I ask the support of all our citizens."

59

Speech draft for remarks upon receiving an honorary degree at Amherst College, Amherst, Massachusetts, October 26, 1963, page 3 showing President Kennedy's handwritten edit

John F. Kennedy Presidential Library and Museum

JFK invited more than 50 writers, painters, poets and musicians to his inauguration—and also invited poet Robert Frost to take part in the inaugural ceremony itself—signaling, from the earliest moments of his administration, that the arts would hold a prominent place in the new government. White House events, designed and meticulously planned by First Lady Jacqueline Kennedy, became a showcase for excellence in American music, dance, theater, and literature during the Kennedy administration.

On October 26, 1963, nearly three years after Robert Frost rang in the Kennedy Presidency with the recital of a poem, the President spoke at the groundbreaking for the library at Amherst College named for Robert Frost. Earlier that day, Amherst presented the President with an honorary degree. In a speech accepting that honor, JFK championed the role of the artist in American life, articulating the principles behind the arts initiatives he and Jacqueline Kennedy were promoting.

Page 3 of the typewritten draft submitted to JFK by Arthur Schlesinger, Special Assistant to the President, is shown here. President Kennedy's edits, handwritten in ink, are transcribed below the page.

high

When power corrupts—poetry cleanses

President Kennedy at the groundbreaking for the Robert Frost Library at Amherst College, October 26, 1963

Courtesy Amherst College Archives & Special Collections

Excerpts from the President's remarks at Amherst College, upon receiving an honorary degree, as delivered October 26, 1963

"Our national strength matters, but the spirit which informs and controls our strength matters just as much.

. . . I look forward to an America which will reward achievement in the arts as we reward achievement in business or statecraft.

. . . And I look forward to an America which commands respect throughout the world not only for its strength but for its civilization as well."

60-63

Family Mementos

In addition to preserving the materials that make up the official record of JFK's Presidency, the Kennedy Library also preserves many of his personal and family belongings. On the centennial anniversary of his birth, a selection of these personal items is displayed for the first time, offering a more private glimpse of the President as a husband and father.

Kennedy crest ring, a gift from the First Lady to the President on his 44th birthday, May 29, 1961

John F. Kennedy Presidential Library and Museum

Two pairs of cufflinks from the President's personal wardrobe

John F. Kennedy Presidential Library and Museum

President Kennedy's sunglasses

John F. Kennedy Presidential Library and Museum

64, 65

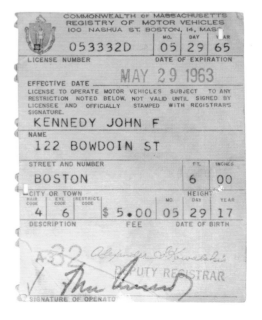

JFK's wallet and Massachusetts driver's license

John F. Kennedy Presidential Library and Museum

66-73

**Neckties and tie clasp from President
Kennedy's personal wardrobe**

John F. Kennedy Presidential Library and Museum

74-76

President Kennedy's cigarette lighter, a cigar from his desk in the Oval Office, and his cigar cutter

John F. Kennedy Presidential Library and Museum

77, 78

Magnifying glass and pencils from the President's desk in the Oval Office

John F. Kennedy Presidential Library and Museum

79, 80

Scrimshaw from President Kennedy's personal collection

John F. Kennedy Presidential Library and Museum

81-83

Two chestnuts found on White House grounds by Caroline and John Jr. and given to their father

John F. Kennedy Presidential Library and Museum

Photographs of President Kennedy with his children, Caroline and John, Jr., and their pony, Macaroni, outside the Oval Office

Courtesy Caroline Kennedy

Drawing by Caroline Kennedy, ca. 1963

John F. Kennedy Presidential Library and Museum

84-97

Many of the photographs shown here are from the Kennedy family's personal collection and include images by Richard Avedon, Mark Shaw and Stanley Tretick, counted among the preeminent photographers of the day.

John F. Kennedy Presidential Library and Museum

99

Undelivered remarks prepared for the Dallas Trade Mart, November 22, 1963, first of 37 speech cards

John F. Kennedy Presidential Library and Museum

President Kennedy was assassinated on November 22, 1963, while riding in an open car, with his wife by his side, during a political trip to Texas. The President's motorcade had been headed to the Dallas Trade Mart, where he was to deliver these remarks to a crowd of more than 2,000 people, members of the Dallas business community and other local leaders.

JFK came to the Presidency with the promise of increasing America's strength in a perilous world. In this undelivered address prefacing his 1964 campaign for re-election, he recapped the advances the nation had made during his time in office.[28]

Dallas Citizens Council, Friday, November 22, 1963

I am honored to have this invitation to address the annual meeting of the Dallas Citizens Council, joined by the members of the Dallas Assembly -- and pleased to have this opportunity to salute the Graduate Research Center of the Southwest.

It is fitting that these two symbols of Dallas progress are united in the sponsorship of this meeting.

98

One of two watercolor paintings of the White House made by Jacqueline Kennedy as a gift for the President, who displayed the pair in the Oval Office. The First Lady signed this one in the lower right hand corner, "J to J."

John F. Kennedy Presidential Library and Museum

"America's leadership must be guided by the lights of learning and reason—or else those who confuse rhetoric with reality and the plausible with the possible will gain the popular ascendancy with their seemingly swift and simple solutions to every world problem.

There will always be dissident voices heard in the land, expressing opposition without alternatives, finding fault but never favor, perceiving gloom on every side and seeking influence without responsibility. Those voices are inevitable.

But today other voices are heard in the land—voices preaching doctrines wholly unrelated to reality, wholly unsuited to the sixties, doctrines which apparently assume that words will suffice without weapons, that vituperation is as good as victory and that peace is a sign of weakness. . . .

We cannot expect that everyone, to use the phrase of a decade ago, will 'talk sense to the American people.' But we can hope that fewer people will listen to nonsense. And the notion that this Nation is headed for defeat through deficit, or that strength is but a matter of slogans, is nothing but just plain nonsense.

I want to discuss with you today the status of our strength and our security because this question clearly calls for the most responsible qualities of leadership and the most enlightened products of scholarship. For this Nation's strength and security are not easily or cheaply obtained, nor are they quickly and simply explained. There are many kinds of strength and no one kind will suffice. Overwhelming nuclear strength cannot stop a guerrilla war. Formal pacts of alliance cannot stop internal subversion. Displays of material wealth cannot stop the disillusionment of diplomats subjected to discrimination.

Above all, words alone are not enough. The United States is a peaceful nation. And where our strength and determination are clear, our words need merely to convey conviction, not belligerence. If we are strong, our strength will speak for itself. If we are weak, words will be of no help.

I realize that this Nation often tends to identify turning-points in world affairs with the major addresses which preceded them. But it was not the Monroe Doctrine that kept all Europe away from this hemisphere--it was the strength of the British fleet and the width of the Atlantic Ocean. It was not General Marshall's speech at Harvard which kept communism out of Western Europe—it was the strength and stability made possible by our military and economic assistance.

In this administration also it has been necessary at times to issue specific warnings—warnings that we could not stand by and watch the Communists conquer Laos by force, or intervene in the Congo, or swallow West Berlin, or maintain offensive missiles on Cuba. But while our goals were at least temporarily obtained in these and other instances, our successful defense of freedom was due not to the words we used, but to the strength we stood ready to use on behalf of the principles we stand ready to defend. . . .

Finally, it should be clear by now that a nation can be no stronger abroad than she is at home. Only an America which practices what it preaches about equal rights and social justice will be respected by those whose choice affects our future. Only an America which has fully educated its citizens is fully capable of tackling the complex problems and perceiving the hidden dangers of the world in which we live. And only an America which is growing and prospering economically can sustain the worldwide defenses of freedom, while demonstrating to all concerned the opportunities of our system and society.

. . . America today is stronger than ever before. Our adversaries have not abandoned their ambitions, our dangers have not diminished, our vigilance cannot be relaxed. But now we have the military, the scientific, and the economic strength to do whatever must be done for the preservation and promotion of freedom.

That strength will never be used in pursuit of aggressive ambitions—it will always be used in pursuit of peace. It will never be used to promote provocations—it will always be used to promote the peaceful settlement of disputes. . . ."

—From President John F. Kennedy's undelivered remarks prepared for the Dallas Trade Mart, November 22, 1963.

100

Portrait of John F. Kennedy by Jamie Wyeth, 1967

Oil on canvas

Courtesy Museum of Fine Arts, Boston. Partial gift of Phyllis and Jamie Wyeth and partial purchase from the Charles H. Bayley Picture and Painting Fund, Emily L. Ainsley Fund, and Robert Jordan Fund

Photograph ©2017 Museum of Fine Arts, Boston

Just a few years after the President's death, members of the Kennedy family asked artist Jamie Wyeth—then age 20—to create a portrait of the late President. Wyeth had never met President Kennedy. Committed to creating an image filled with life, the artist studied biographies, photographs, and film footage of JFK and spoke at length with the President's widow. He also observed and closely studied the mannerisms of the President's brothers, Robert and Ted, creating drawings and sketches of the two from life in an attempt to capture family traits. He even created a portrait of Ted Kennedy on this very canvas, which he eventually transformed into the President's likeness. Wyeth later recalled, "I was so desperate. I didn't want it to look like a posthumous painting."[29]

"*We in this country, in this generation, are—by destiny rather than choice—the watchmen on the walls of world freedom. We ask, therefore, that we may be worthy of our power and responsibility, that we may exercise our strength with wisdom and restraint, and that we may achieve in our time and for all time the ancient vision of 'peace on earth, good will toward men.'*
That must always be our goal, and the righteousness of our cause must always underlie our strength. For as was written long ago: 'except the Lord keep the city, the watchman waketh but in vain.'"

—From President John F. Kennedy's undelivered remarks prepared for the Dallas Trade Mart, November 22, 1963

Endnotes

1 "Statement by the President Upon Signing Order Establishing the Peace Corps," March 1, 1961. *Public Papers of the Presidents, John F. Kennedy, Containing the Public Messages, Speeches, and Statements of the President, 1961.* Washington, DC: U.S. Government Printing Office, 1962, p. 135.

2 "Remarks in the Rudolph Wilde Platz, Berlin," June 26, 1963. *Public Papers of the Presidents, John F. Kennedy, Containing the Public Messages, Speeches, and Statements of the President, January 1 to November 22, 1963.* Washington, DC: U.S. Government Printing Office, 1964, p. 525.

3 "Message of the Boys of '61 to the Boys of '17," *Boston Globe*, May 29, 1917, Evening Edition, p. 1.

4 Nese R. DeBruyne and Anne Leland, "American War and Military Operations Casualties: Lists and Statistics," *Congressional Research Service*, January 2, 2015, RL32492, https://fas.org/sgp/crs/natsec/RL32492.pdf; also John W. Chambers, II, ed. in chief, *The Oxford Companion to American Military History.* New York, NY: Oxford University Press, 1999, p. 849.

5 "Every Kitchen Must Be Mobilized," *Boston Daily Globe*, May 29, 1917, p. 6.

6 "Mob of 3,000 Rules in East St. Louis, Attack and Beat Imported Negro Workers—Police and Militia Unable to Control Rioters." *New York Times*, May 29, 1917.

7 "War Department Calls for Student Aviators," *Boston Daily Globe*, May 29, 1917, p. 9.

8 https://ia802703.us.archive.org/10/items/TheUSAirServiceInWWIVol1/TheUSAirServiceInWWIVol1.pdf, p. 93.

9 "Red Sox Play Double-Header," *Boston Globe*, May 29, 1917, Evening Edition, p. 1.

10 Audio tour of John F. Kennedy National Historic Site, 83 Beals Street, Brookline, MA, National Park Service.

11 Pitts, David. *Jack and Lem: John F. Kennedy and Lem Billings—The Untold Story of an Extraordinary Friendship*. New York: Carroll & Graf Publishers, 2007, p. 13.

12 "Gertrude Stein and *The Lit*" http://self.gutenberg.org/articles/eng/Choate_School#Gertrude_Stein_and_The_Lit.

13 "The President's Best Friend," by David Michaelis, *American Heritage*, June/July 1983, Volume 34, Issue 4.

14 "Awaits Papa's Blessing—Mrs. Warren Johnson, the former Ruth Moffett," *New York Post*, January 20, 1936.

15 Post by Greg Bradsher: https://prologue.blogs.archives.gov/2012/09/24/john-f-kennedy-and-pt-boat-59; also Joseph Hinds, "JFK's Other PT Boat Rescue," *America in WWII*, February 2011; also, Graham, James W. *Victura: The Kennedys, a Sailboat, and the Sea*, Lebanon, NH: Fore Edge, 2014, pp. 73-74.

16 Dallek, Robert. *An Unfinished Life—John F. Kennedy, 1917-1963*. Boston, New York, London: Little, Brown and Company, 2003, p. 165.

17 Kennedy, John F. *Profiles in Courage*. New York, NY: Harper & Brothers, Publishers, 1956, p. 245.

18 Executive Order 10914, Providing for an Expanded Program of Food Distribution to Needy Families, January 21, 1961, National Archives and Records Administration, Record Group 11.

19 *Saturday Evening Post*, March 1958.

20 *Eleanor Roosevelt Papers Project:* https://www2.gwu.edu/~erpapers/mep/displaydoc.cfm?docid=jfk58.

21 Tye, Larry. *Bobby Kennedy: The Making of a Liberal Icon*, New York, NY: Random House, 2016, p. 128.

22 Dictabelt Conversation 39, Fall 1960, President's Office Files, Presidential Recordings Collection, John F. Kennedy Presidential Library and Museum.

23 "Fabian Bachrach, 92, Portraitist Who Photographed Kennedy, Dies," by Margalit Fox, *New York Times*, March 1, 2010.

24 Sorensen, Theodore, C. *Kennedy*, Old Saybrook, CT: Konecky & Konecky, 1965, p. 309.

25 "Kennedy Talked, Khrushchev Triumphed," by Nathan Thrall and Jesse James Wilkins, *New York Times*, May 22, 2008.

26 John H. Glenn Oral History Interview, JFK #1, 6/12/1964, John F. Kennedy Oral History Collection, John F. Kennedy Presidential Library and Museum.

27 http://www.tuscaloosanews.com/news/20130117/james-hood-one-of-the-first-black-students-at-the-university-of-alabama-dies; also "James Hood, Who Integrated University of Alabama, Dies at 70," *Washington Post*, January 18, 2013.

28 Clarke, Thurston. *JFK's Last Hundred Days—The Transformation of a Man and the Emergence of a Great President*, New York, NY: The Penguin Press, p. 341.

29 Interview with Jared Bowen, *PBS Newshour*, August 10, 2014.